The Scientist's
Guide to Physics™

Discovering the Nature of

Energy

Nora Clemens
and Robert Greenberger

ROSEN
PUBLISHING®

New York

Published in 2012 by The Rosen Publishing Group, Inc.
29 East 21st Street, New York, NY 10010

First Edition

Library of Congress Cataloging-in-Publication Data

Clemens, Nora.
Discovering the nature of energy / Nora Clemens, Robert Greenberger.—1st ed.
    p. cm.—(The scientist's guide to physics)
Includes bibliographical references and index.
ISBN 978-1-4488-4702-0 (library binding)
1. Force and energy—Juvenile literature. I. Greenberger, Robert. II. Title.
QC73.4.C5168 2012
621.042—dc22

                                            2010049960

Manufactured in the United States of America

CPSIA Compliance Information: Batch #S11YA: For further information, contact Rosen Publishing, New York, New York, at 1-800-237-9932.

Contents

INTRODUCTION

What is energy? Scientists define it as the ability to perform work, and work is defined as moving an object a certain distance by applying a certain force. We often think of energy as an object with mass, as if we could hold a certain amount of energy in our hands. You can do this, after a fashion, if you pick up a battery. Yet even that really isn't energy.

A radio wave moving through empty space consists of energy, electromagnetic energy, but you cannot hold the wave in your hand. The only reason we know that the energy is there is because at some point the wave strikes the antenna of a radio receiver, and this causes electrons in the radio's circuits to move. If the electrons move, work has been performed, and therefore energy has been transferred to those electrons.

There is an intimate relationship between energy and motion. One form of energy, kinetic energy, is defined as the energy of motion. Objects that move have this energy, and if they struck other objects they would impart some of their motion to those objects, performing work on them.

Other objects have potential energy, that is, they may not be moving, but there are forces acting on them that could cause them to move. A boulder resting at the edge of a high cliff has potential energy because it feels the force of gravity from below. If it were pushed off the edge of the cliff, it would accelerate and move toward the ground, performing work by creating an impact crater in the earth.

Heat energy is defined as the motion or oscillations of the atoms and molecules that make up a substance. The more motion, the more heat energy. This heat energy can be transferred to other materials, making their atoms and molecules vibrate with greater motion.

The more kinds of energy we examine, the more we see that the potential to cause an object to move is at the heart of the definition of energy. In fact, one form of energy can be transformed into another form of energy by imparting movement to an object.

So, energy is not so much an object as a measure of the amount of work that can be performed, or the motion that can be transferred from one object to another. The more we learn about energy, the more efficiently we are able to harness its value. We're constantly discovering new ways to use the vast energy resources of our planet to channel the power that we need to survive.

IN THE BEGINNING

Chapter 1

Energy has always been present on Earth, but it took man millennia to start giving its source and nature any serious consideration. After all, man had to worry about food, shelter, and fending off predatory animals until he began to form tribes and communities. At the least, early humans knew that the sun was warm, and when it went away, it grew cold, hence the need for shelter.

To fill in the answers, man created myths—stories of gods and goddesses, some human, some less so, who brought Earth into existence. An angry god brought about a storm, while a loving god made the plants grow. A study of mythology shows how most

civilizations divided up events, ascribing them to various deities.

In reality, nature provided fire whenever lightning struck a flammable object such as a tree. Eventually, the first humans recognized that fire provided heat, something that didn't vanish after the sun set. The flames also provided light, and soon fire was coveted and ingenious people found ways to keep fires and their embers from going out. It was perhaps the first precious commodity used for trade. Tending the fire, according to anthropologists, became a new job for the elderly, who could no longer hunt, or the young, who were learning the ways of the tribe.

Over time, humans figured out how to start their own fires, rather than nurture the same flame or wait for a thunderstorm. With this step came the ability to light multiple places and even to start cooking the animal flesh they brought back to the group. Anthropologists have been able to study skeletons and partially preserved bodies, allowing them to conclude that cooked food was more agreeable to these early people's tastes.

Before science could decode the nature of energy, civilizations explained the mysteries of nature through supernatural beings, such as Prometheus, the Greek god who brought fire to mankind.

ANCIENT TIMES

As humankind developed, one source of energy was harnessed after another. After fire, most likely came wind, as records show that man had the first sailboats in use some 5,000 years ago. Then, wind was used to power equipment with windmills developed 2,500 years ago. In 800 CE, Muslims were the first to have windmills turn large stones to grind grains.

Greece, considered the center of modern learning, was one place where the true nature of things was first pondered. Thales of Miletus (624–548 BCE) is considered the first to have made observations and record them, rather than ascribe acts to the gods. He rubbed amber with a cloth and noted how the wool stuck, the first true observation of static electricity. He also came to the conclusion that water was the primordial element from which all other activity sprang. Thales noted how it was present everywhere: it fell from the sky, quenched people's thirst, and sustained the fish they would eat. He rejected the popular notion that gods were responsible for the way things

About 2,500 years ago, thinkers such as Thales of Miletus, Heraclitus, and Anaximenes (pictured) began to give more scientific explanations about the nature of energy than ever before.

worked. He believed the world worked in cycles, with causes and effects.

Anaximenes (570–500 BCE) declared air was the principal element in the universe. Whereas Thales concluded the land floated atop water, Anaximenes saw air in the land, in the sky, everywhere. He noted how air condensed to become rain or snow and how we needed it to breathe.

Fire was the primal element, declared Heraclitus of Ephesus (540–480 BCE). According to him, fire ruled the world, condensing the water or heating the air. To his credit, he was also the first to see how these various elements reacted toward one another, calling it a "struggle between opposites." After pondering how things interact, he concluded, "We must realize that discord is common to all things, that justice results from struggle and that all things are born and disappear through strife."

Interestingly, Anaxagoras (610–547 BCE), a student of Thales's, rejected the notion of water being the primal element. Instead, he had his own theories about an all-encompassing force in nature. It wasn't until Empedocles of Agrigentum (490–435 BCE) that anyone tried to unify the various elements. He took Thales's belief about water being the central element to life and combined that with the competing views of contemporaries: Anaximenes favoring air, Heraclitus fire, and Xenophanes (570–475 BCE) earth.

Empedocles concluded that everything was made up of these four elements, in differing proportions. Being a mystic, he saw the forces of change as being human will, love, or strife rather than natural changes. Empedocles was typical of his day: he embodied fervent spiritual belief along with the quest to understand the world around him. He took this all to an extreme, however, when he hurled himself into Mount Etna to prove he was a god. He did, though, firmly establish the idea of four elements—earth, air, water, and fire—and left it to other thinkers to build on these ideas.

Around the world, during these early centuries of humankind's development, different natural resources were tapped and, after some experimentation, put into everyday use. Archaeologists have determined that man regularly started using wood for fire during the Stone Age, some 25,000 years ago. While the Greeks considered the forces of nature nearly 3,000 years ago, the Egyptians found that the oil atop ponds could be burned for light. In the Far East, the Chinese had discovered that ignited natural gas could help extract salt from the sea. In North America, the Native Americans used the abundant resources of coal to make fire, which led to heat, light, cooking, and making pottery. The most common item used for burning was wood, a fact that remained unchanged until the nineteenth century. Meanwhile in the Middle East, fire was also employed to heat minerals dug

ENERGY STORAGE IN THE ANCIENT WORLD

Khujut Rabu, a region just outside Baghdad, Iraq, yielded an earthenware jar that mystified archaeologists when first examined. German archaeologist Wilhelm König was the first to describe the object in 1938, just as World War II (1939–1945) was breaking out across Europe. As a result, his conclusions were not fully absorbed by the scientific community until much later.

The jar, dating back about 2,000 years, seems to be the world's first battery. The jar had an asphalt stopper with an iron rod stuck through the stopper. Inside, a copper cylinder surrounded the iron rod. König's suggestion that this was an electric battery went unnoticed until the war's conclusion. It fell to General Electric's high voltage lab in Pittsfield, Massachusetts, to build re-creations for study. Willard F. M. Gray filled one such prototype with grape juice, similar to what might have been used two millennia ago. The electrolyte-filled liquid managed to produce two volts of power.

Why had the they built such a device? What was it used for? The Parthians, who lived in the region where the jar was found, were known not as scientists but as warriors. Theories include that they obtained it from a different community, perhaps a spoil of combat.

from the ground. Metals such as tin and copper were heated to a high melting temperature and formed into weapons and tools.

The Far East was also making interesting discoveries about energy. In China, the first magnetic rocks were discovered and put to use. Slivers of this rock were eventually used to form the first compasses and enable navigation. The Chinese also are credited with first using coal to smelt copper, about 1000 BCE. Coal became preferable to wood since it burned more slowly and generated more heat.

Europeans learned of coal when Marco Polo returned from exploring China in 1295. The Netherlands was the first site of digging and extracting these black stones from the earth, and trade with other countries soon followed. Eventually, mining coal for energy became prevalent in other countries throughout Europe. Wood was then saved for construction of homes and ships, as trade by sea became increasingly practical. People tolerated the soot and smog caused by burning tons of coal every day.

The Renaissance

The next significant era of scientific inquiry into energy occurred during the European Renaissance, starting with early astronomer Johannes Kepler (1571–1630). He recognized that there was a harmony among the elements, which he ascribed to God's perfection. Much of his study involved the planets and the stars, beginning with the Greeks' beliefs, with the addition of his own notions. After a time, he developed the three laws of planetary motion:

- The orbits of the planets are ellipses, with the sun at one focus of the ellipse.
- The line joining the planet to the sun sweeps out equal areas in equal times as the planet travels around the ellipse.
- The ratio of the squares of the revolutionary periods for two planets is equal to the ratio of the cubes of their semi-major axes.

The laws were assigned specifically to planets and no other heavenly bodies. Kepler presented these laws as fact without any explanation for why they worked. Kepler made other important contributions to math and science, including work on optics and the first correct theory of how the human eye works.

Two thousand years after Anaximenes, astronomer Johannes Kepler revolutionized our understanding of the heavens with his breakthrough discoveries on the nature of planetary motion.

CAP.
XXIV.

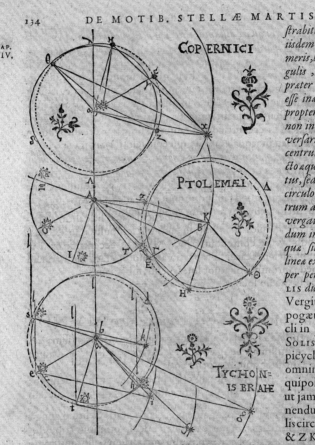

COPERNICI

PTOLEMÆI

TYCHO=
NIS BRAHE

strabitur (ut prius) iisdem plane numeris, lineis & angulis, has lineas præter opinionem, esse inæquales, ac propterea Martem non in circulo Γ Δ versari, cujus sit centrum in K puncto æqualitatis motus, sed in Z E H Θ circulo, cujus centrum a K versus B vergat, propemodum in linea K B. quæ sit parallelos lineæ ex A TERRA per perigæum SOLIS ductæ.

Vergit igitur apogæum epicycli in perigæum SOLIS. Et quia epicyclus propter omnimodam æquipollentiam, ut jam dictū, ponendus est æqualis circuitui Solis, & Z K parallelos ipsi Ξ A, & EK ipsi O A, & HK ipsi I A, & ΘK ipsi T A: igitur etiam ipsas Ξ A, O A, I A, T A, inæquales esse verisimile est: & punctum medii loci SOLIS (BRAHEANA notione centrum epicycli SOLIS) per circuitum a puncto æqualitatis distare inæqualiter. Quod obiter interjeci. nihil .n. facit ad præsentem demonstrationem, nisi quod eam extendit amplius.

In forma TYCHONICA *sit A* TERRA, *& ex ea scribatur* SOLIS *concentricus* C D, *qui putetur esse deferens* SYSTEMA *Planetarum; cum sit A punctum æqualitatis motus concentrici* SOLIS. *Erit itaque* SOL *ipse in alio eccentrico circulo. Sit ejus centrum ab A versus partes B. Sit autem A L regula lineæ apsidum* MARTIS, *ut linea apsidum circulatione & transpositione sui eccentrici semper maneat parallelos ipsi A L. Sint autem lineæ medii motus* SOLIS *ad nostra quatuor momenta* A H, A T, A E, A S: *& ex A ejiciantur lineæ visionum* MARTIS, *prout supra descriptæ sunt, in hunc vel illum zodiaci gradum vergere. Et quia ponitur* MARS *omnibus quatuor vicibus eodem*

Galileo Galilei (1564–1642), an Italian philosopher and astronomer, is considered by many to be the true founder of physics, but he was really one of several contemporaries who put aside the era's religious fervor in favor of rational thought. He synthesized theories put forth centuries earlier by Archimedes and Aristotle, including them in his *Disclosure on Bodies in Water*. His study of motion and rest led to his concept of inertia: an object in motion will remain in motion until acted upon by an outside force. He experimented with a small ball being rolled between two inclines. As he adjusted the angle of incline, he measured how long it took the ball to travel the same distance. The results proved his theory of inertia and would become Isaac Newton's first law of motion. Galileo also concluded through his telescopic observations of the moon that matter making up Earth's surface is the same as on other bodies in space. This idea was in exact opposition of the accepted belief of the day that heavenly bodies such as the moon were smooth and perfect, with no craters or mountains.

THE THREE LAWS OF MOTION

Sir Isaac Newton (1642–1727) built on the ideas of Kepler, Galileo, and others in developing physical laws. While today he is best remembered for the legend of the falling apple leading to the "discovery" of gravity, he had a much greater impact on scientific thought and development.

Newton began to study law at Trinity College in Cambridge, Great Britain, until he was exposed to the writings of Galileo and Kepler. Newton then went on to write his own thoughts in his 1664 book *Quaestiones Quaedam Philosophicae* (*Certain Philosophical Questions*). To fully focus on mathematics, Newton put his law studies aside. Starting with Euclid, he read all accounts available. He completed these studies in 1665, and within two years, his work astounded the world. He invented the foundations of the mathematical discipline of calculus, independent of Germany's Gottfried von Leibniz.

Kepler gave a geometric description of planetary orbits, but Newton would explain why planets moved at different speeds at different points in their orbits. Newton's observations and use of new mathematical concepts electrified the world of thinkers in the seventeenth century. His laws of motion are as follows:

First Law of Motion: An object at rest or in uniform motion in a straight line will remain at rest or in the same uniform motion unless

acted upon by an unbalanced force. This is also known as the law of inertia.

Second Law of Motion: The acceleration of an object is directly proportional to the total unbalanced force exerted on the object, and is inversely proportional to the mass of the object (in other words, as mass increases, the acceleration has to decrease). The acceleration of an object moves in the same direction as the total force. This is also known as the law of acceleration: force = mass × acceleration ($F = ma$).

Third Law of Motion: If one object exerts a force on a second object, the second object exerts a force equal in magnitude and opposite in direction on the object body. This is also known as the law of interaction.

By joining his second and third laws, Newton was able to derive conservation of momentum, which he demonstrated and measured with collisions of

Considered one of the greatest scientists of all time, Sir Isaac Newton changed the way we think about the nature of energy by devising his three laws of motion, which are fundamental to the science of physics.

pendulums. If two bodies exert equal and opposite force on one another, then the rate of change of momentum in either must be the same.

These laws became important building blocks in understanding energy. In addition, Newton developed the theory of universal gravitation and demonstrated that Kepler's laws follow the law of gravitation. In fact, Newton went even further: he showed that Kepler's laws of planetary motion were only approximately correct and supplied the quantitative corrections that made these measurements more precise.

USING ENERGY

Chapter

2

ewton's many accomplishments provided a strong foundation for his contemporaries and those who followed. They also had the benefit of inspiring others to question, observe, notate, and publish the results. Yet what practical effects did this provide? By now, it had long been accepted that the planet's substances worked together and in opposition to one another, and the resulting combinations provided heat, light, motion, and life itself. For example: fire generates heat, changing the air from cool to warm, and as it heats up, the water might condense, changing to steam. This change of form was just now being harnessed to create energy.

THOMAS SAVERY

One of the first to take all that learning and apply it to help the common man was Thomas Savery (ca. 1650–1715), an English engineer. With much of the land deforested, the remaining wood was needed for the growing navy and for home construction. Much of the fuel for heating these homes came from coal, but mining the mineral proved slow, especially because water had to be drained from mines. Savery learned from Otto von Guericke (1602–1686), a German physicist, about vacuums and the first air pump. He wanted to adapt the air pump and find a way to power it to remove the water from mines, speeding up the entire process. Savery's goal was to generate the vacuum required for the pump to function by using steam to fill the device and then condense it. Called the Miner's Friend, the invention was the first practical water pump proving the ability to convert one form of energy to another. This required such high pressure and generated such heat that it risked

In the seventeenth and eighteenth centuries, tools such as the Miner's Friend were being utilized by humankind to harness energy.

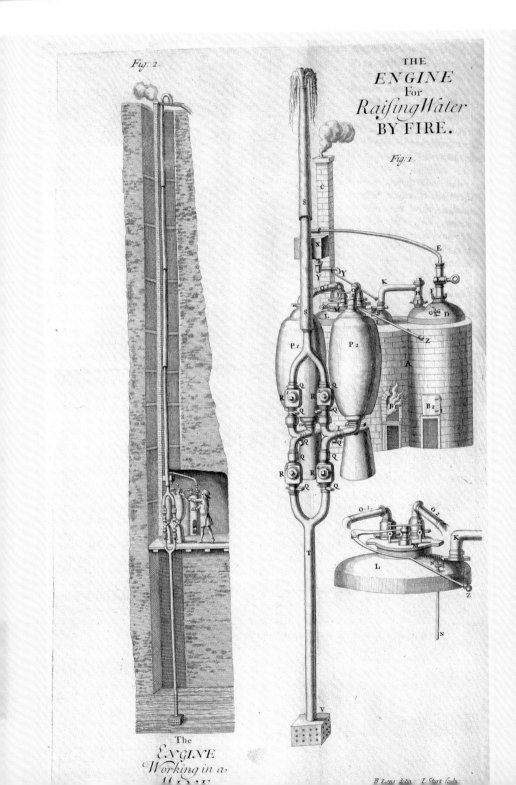

Fig. 2.

THE
ENGINE
For
Raifing Water
BY FIRE.

Fig. 1.

The
ENGINE
Working in a
MINE

B. Lens delin.   I. Sturt Sculp.

explosions, and thus, the invention was not widely used. Advanced engineering was needed to make Savery's invention practical.

Savery's invention was improved upon by Thomas Newcomen (1663–1729), an engineer who rejected high-pressure steam in favor of atmospheric pressure. Newcomen developed the piston and cylinder system—pistons, placed in airtight, high-polished cylinders, would be pushed in and out by the change of air pressure. This created the energy required to power the machinery. Newcomen entered into a partnership with Savery, and they had their first machine in operation by 1712. More successful than the Miner's Friend, it was in common use by 1725, the precursor to the coming Industrial Revolution.

Turning Steam Into Energy

Scottish chemist Joseph Black (1728–1799) helped determine how much energy existed when water was turned to steam. He measured water turning to ice as well as to steam, noting the temperature changes. Black noted that the heat taken up in one change was given off in the reverse change, a fundamental principal in the conservation of energy.

USING THE OCEAN'S ENERGY

The sun's heating of ocean water, condensing it into steam, can be harnessed as thermal energy. Given the depths of the oceans, the sun's radiation can reach only so far. The temperature difference between the warmed waters and the cooler, deeper waters is the thermal energy. The U.S. Department of Energy has described this as being enough to power the entire world, if ever tapped. The thermal energy could generate electricity in one of three cycles: closed, open, and hybrid. A closed system uses the solar-heated water to boil a fluid with a low boiling point, such as ammonia. As the vapor expands, the engine could be operated. The open cycle actually boils the seawater, creating the steam to power an engine. The hybrid cycle uses a combination of both open and closed cycles to produce the steam for an engine.

Thermal energy is a far more constant source of energy in a fixed place than the mechanical energy derived from tides and waves (which are generated by wind). A dam known as a barrage is used to take tidal energy and force the water through turbines to work a generator. Waves can be turned into energy through three methods: channel systems that funnel the waves into reservoirs, float systems that power hydraulic pumps, and the oscillating water column system that uses the waves to compress air within a contained space.

Several decades later, in 1769, Sir Richard Arkwright (1732–1792) introduced a machine that built upon Savery and Newcomen's work. He created a device that replicated hand motion for the making of textiles and at first powered it with horses. He switched to falling water and finally, in 1790, to steam. This proved so efficient that he put many people out of work, helping usher in the Industrial Revolution as machines took over repetitious work.

As machines began displacing laborers, there was fear and more than a little rebellion. Factories and their owners were targets of protests and riots. In March 1811, the English textile factories became the sites of the first Luddite riots. Taking their name from their leader, Ned Ludd, the Luddites began a six-year wave of attacks across England. They sought to destroy the powered machines that displaced them and to end wage reductions. The government made such destruction of machines a capital offense in 1812, and it took an economic crisis in 1817 to bring the revolt to an end. Today, "Luddite" refers to a person who fears technological change.

James Watt (1736–1819) of Scotland was the next inventor to truly build upon the principals of

Scottish inventor James Watt was able to create efficiencies within a steam engine that revolutionized the way people transported goods.

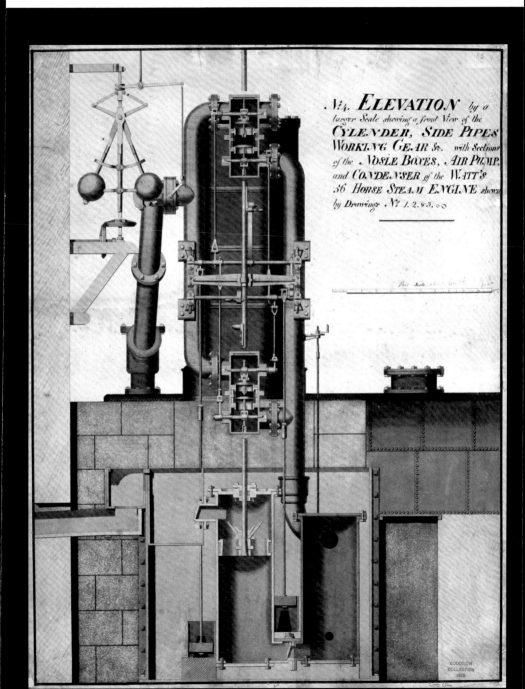

James Watt's breakthroughs in the study of energy arguably brought about the Industrial Revolution.

physics. Watt was trained to be an instrument maker but was unable to meet the rigid requirements to work at his craft. Instead, he retreated to teach at the University of Glasgow. There, Watt met Joseph Black, who taught him about the construction and repair of steam engines. In 1764, Watt was then given a Newcomen steam engine to repair. He took it apart and began to apply the lessons he had learned from Black to improve the engine. The greatest inefficiency, he learned, was the constant heating and cooling in the same chamber to produce the steam and vacuum. Watt developed a second chamber, called the condenser, which would hold the cold while the cylinder was kept hot. By not canceling each other out, more energy was retained for the machine itself. The creation of the second chamber also enabled the piston to be moved from two directions, not one, which generated more speed and, thus, more power.

Black was impressed with the developments and funded the work. Within five years, Watt had improved the steam engine. It was such a success that he entered a partnership with a businessman in 1774, and by 1800, more than 500 were in use. He went on to patent the rotary engine, the double-action engine, and the steam indicator—all of which benefited manufacturing.

Watt measured a horse's ability to pull a 150-pound (68-kg) weight in 1783, concluding the weight could be raised 4 feet (1.2 meters) in a second. He used this measure of "horse power" in describing the output of his engine, a term that remains in use to this day. Another measure in the metric system was later named after the inventor, the watt. One unit of horsepower equals 746 watts.

By 1784, Watt had used his principles to also create steam heating pipes with which to warm his office. So, not only did Watt build the first truly viable steam engine, he also created what is known today as steam heat.

Engines heated by coal instead of water produced the same effect and freed manufacturers from having to be located near ready supplies of water. The size of these engines and the machines they powered would increase over the years, fueling the Industrial Revolution in England, then throughout Europe before reaching the fledgling United States.

Historians consider Watt's engine to be the first truly modern machine. Its power was such that it transformed one business after another, which made manufacturing cheaper and more efficient. It also put people out of work, so it was reviled and threatened on numerous occasions by those it replaced. Cities were built around these factories, changing societies in ways that included the rapid decline of farming and the rise of slums. The black smoke belching from these factories also caused the first serious problem of air pollution. People lived with the darkened skies, smelly air, and lingering soot as the price for earning a livelihood in this new era of progress.

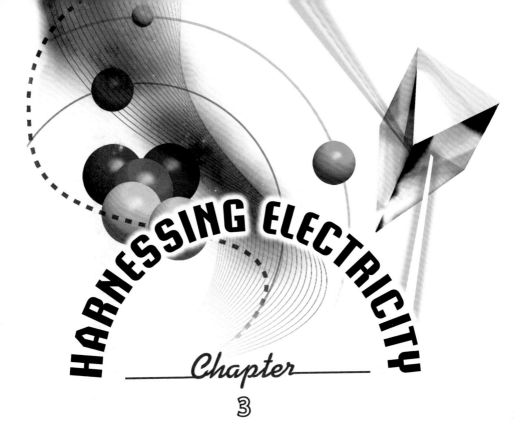

HARNESSING ELECTRICITY

Chapter 3

The innovative Thales of Miletus had been the first to record any observations regarding static electricity. While others pursued different lines of inquiry, Thales questioned this sparking and wondered how it might be harnessed. However, it took centuries before any practical conclusions were drawn.

William Gilbert (1544–1603), a physician, would name those charges. Gilbert was renowned for his brilliance and constant experimentation. The great Italian physicist and astronomer Galileo even acknowledged him as the founder of "experimentalism."

The next frontier in energy was electricity. Dutch physicist Pieter van Musschenbroek and Otto von Guericke broke ground in this field with a device that produced static electricity.

While Gilbert's work concentrated mostly on magnetism and the discovery of Earth's magnetic poles, he made the distinction between this and the static charges, or, "electrics"—the term he derived from the Greek word for amber, *elektron*.

Pieter van Musschenbroek

Nearly a century later, the work of Dutch physicist Pieter van Musschenbroek (1692–1761) with static electricity would revolutionize the study of energy. Previous to him, Otto von Guericke had developed a sulfur globe atop a crank-turned shaft that could store and discharge static electricity. By building upon Gilbert's discoveries, von Guericke opened up an entirely new field of study, upon which van Musschenbroek capitalized.

In one such experiment, he filled a metal container with water, placed a brass wire in one end, stuck the other end through a piece of cork, and then built up a static charge. When his assistant picked up the exposed brass wire, he received the first artificially produced electric shock.

Subsequently, it was learned that when a fully charged object is placed near another metal object, a spark would leap from metal to metal. Since this occurred at the University of Leiden in January 1746, the metal object was named the Leiden jar and became a popular item for physicists around Europe.

Later, the Leiden jar was modified and renamed a condenser by Alessandro Volta. Poland's Ewald Georg von Kleist (1700–1748) also developed the jar concept at the same time, although he, not an assistant, suffered the shock.

Benjamin Franklin is perhaps the most well-known experimenter of electricity. In a June thunderstorm in 1752, he famously channeled the storm's electrical energy using a kite and a key.

BENJAMIN FRANKLIN

In America, Benjamin Franklin (1706–1790) also worked with the jar. He was the first scientist to equate the spark with lightning. This led to the historic experiment with the kite, wire, and thunderstorm in June 1752. At the end of the wire was a silk thread, and attached to the thread was a metal key. As with the Leiden jar, when he put his hand near the key, it sparked. He then charged a jar from the energized key, proving that lightning naturally produced electricity. Unfortunately, the next two men to repeat the experiment were electrocuted. Franklin was then inducted into England's Royal Society.

Franklin's work led to the development of the lightning rod, which attracted lightning away from the wooden buildings of the day, protecting them from natural disaster. His study also led to his proposal that there existed two kinds of electricity, positive and negative. This furthered the understanding of the raw power available, but no one was sure what could be done with it.

Franklin, while in England protesting the taxation of Americans in 1766, met Joseph Priestley (1733–1804) and inspired the young man to study electricity. Priestley discovered that carbon was an electrical conductor and wrote, in 1769, a history on the subject of electricity. He theorized that electricity would be important in the development of chemistry and he turned his attention to that field.

LUIGI GALVANI

Another person studying the Leiden jars was Italy's Luigi Galvani (1737–1798), an anatomist. Sparks from his lab's Leiden jar caused dissected frogs' legs to twitch. Further study showed that the legs twitched when exposed to thunderstorms as well as when they made contact with two different metals. While Galvani believed in a then-popular notion known as animal electricity, he was later proven wrong by Alessandro Volta. Still, his work immortalized him with the word "galvanized" being used to describe the steady electricity set up by two metals in contact with one another. A galvanometer is an instrument to detect electric current and was so named in his honor by André Ampère.

THE ROYAL SOCIETY

The Royal Society was founded on November 28, 1660, years after local scientists had begun meeting weekly to share their new discoveries and philosophies. Among the first dozen to join were the noted astronomy professor and architect Christopher Wren, Robert Boyle, John Wilkins, and Sir Robert Moray. They continued to meet weekly and demonstrated experiments for one another across the scientific spectrum. Upon learning of this group, King Charles II gave it his approval. The society quickly developed a library of learning and then a museum, gaining international prestige for being the first organization of its kind in Europe. Rules for admission were established, and over time they were refined until recommendations had to be in writing and subject to rigorous review. As a result, it became an elite organization with membership denoting achievement of the highest regard in the scientific community.

The Leiden jar was a device that illustrated that an electrical spark could leap from one metal object to another.

Priestley's history of electricity proved inspirational to Alessandro Giuseppe Volta (1745–1827). A professor of physics in his native Como, Italy, Volta developed the next generation condenser, surpassing the Leiden jar. What he devised involved a resin-coated metal plate and a second plate with an insulated handle. The resin plate is rubbed to develop a charge, which by then was known to be a negative charge. The second plate is placed over it and the negative charge is repelled to the top while the positive charge is drawn to the bottom of the second plate. The negative charge could then be drawn off the top plate through grounding, letting the insulated, handled plate build up a strong positive charge. These works were celebrated, and he was inducted into the Royal Society in 1791.

Following Galvani's work, Volta came to learn that the electric charges were not produced by any unique animal energy but by other means. While this embittered Galvani, Volta went on to determine more about electric charges. Using bowls of salt solution and a dripping metal arc—the metal tipped with copper at one end and zinc at the other—he managed to sustain a steady flow of electricity. By this time, such items were used in a device called a battery. This became the first electric battery. Over time, Volta refined and miniaturized the battery, substituting discs of metal instead of arcs. One such battery consisted of copper at the bottom followed by zinc, and then cardboard soaked in the solution, with repetitions of the copper, zinc, and cardboard combination. With a wire attached to the top and bottom of the battery, an electric current would pass through the circuit. His peers in the scientific community chose to name the measure of electronic force the volt.

The Dawn of Electrodynamics

When Danish physicist Hans Christian Ørsted (1777–1851) discovered that a wire carrying a current could deflect a compass needle, scientists throughout

Europe immediately went to work. André-Marie Ampère (1775–1836) came up with important news about electric current. Building on Ørsted's work and on Franklin's notion of positive and negative charges, he determined the course of the current based on the shape of the metal. Ampère felt that if a current in a wire exerted a magnetic force on a compass needle, two such wires should also interact magnetically. He showed that this interaction was simple and fundamental—parallel currents attract, non-parallel currents repel. The force between two long straight parallel currents was inversely proportional to the distance between them and proportional to the intensity of the current flowing in each.

This opened up the new science of studying electric current, known as electrodynamics, by Ampère. Later, Lord Kelvin, who will be discussed in the next chapter, named the measure of electric current passing a given point amperes. Overall, Ampère's work led scientists to continue their studies in new and unique ways, while inventors tried to tap in to what could be done with this new power.

Sir Humphrey Davy (1778–1829) provided the first answer. A chemist by trade, he was intrigued by the successful use of electricity to break up a water molecule. He began studying what an electric charge would do with other substances. In 1805,

Davy developed an electric arc that so impressed Napoléon Bonaparte, he was awarded a prize for best work of the year. Despite England and France being at war, Davy went to Napoléon's France to accept the medal, noting that scientists were never at war. He then went on to construct the world's largest battery, using over 250 metal plates to store a massive charge. The charge was then applied to liquid solutions such as lime, magnesia, and potash, or wood ash, which are suspected of containing metallic components. On October 7, 1807, Davy succeeded in liberating a substance from potash, which he named potassium. The water molecule was separated from the potash, combining with the oxygen and became the new substance, while the escaping hydrogen became a visible violet flame. A week later, he managed the same with soda (sodium carbonate).

Once word spread, others imitated his work, and within months, several people were isolating new elements using Davy's method. These early nineteenth-century discoveries catapulted man's knowledge of chemistry.

Before Davy died, his body ravaged by exposure to so many airborne chemicals, Davy took his electric arc and applied it to illumination for the first time. His arc lamp was developed to aid miners and paved the way to Thomas Edison's lightbulb.

MICHAEL FARADAY

During Davy's studies, he received a series of drawings from Michael Faraday (1791–1867), a young man desperate to secure work in the sciences. Faraday grew up poor, one of ten children, and was unable to get a proper education. He was fortunate to be apprenticed to a bookbinder where he was exposed to various writings. A customer gave Faraday a ticket to hear Davy lecture and the young man was captivated.

In 1813, Faraday became an assistant to Davy. In time, Faraday grew to greater prominence than Davy, with the older man resenting the student's praises. Faraday built upon and surpassed his mentor in several fields, most notably chemistry and electronics. It was Faraday, for example, who coined the name "electrolysis" for the process of extracting metals from molten compounds, which he termed electrolytes. The metal rods inserted into the electrolytes were named electrodes; a positive electrode was named the anode, a negative one was named a cathode.

Work continued on electricity's many properties and its close relationship to magnetism. William Sturgeon (1783–1850) was the first to meld electricity and magnetism. He took Ampère's coiled metal, known as a solenoid, and wrapped it around iron, then sent a charge through it. This created a magnetic attraction that pulled twenty times its own weight and was the world's first electromagnet.

Inspired by Ørsted's work, Faraday went into the lab and developed a line of reasoning entirely independent of Davy. He created a device involving metal bars and two containers of mercury. Faraday's research led to the discovery of the reverse effect, the production of electric current by magnetism. With a current attached, he managed to prove that electric and magnetic forces could be harnessed for continual mechanical movement.

This first electric motor was considered a scientific toy, with no one then realizing how this could be applied beyond the lab. Further work also combined the research of Ampère and Sturgeon, proving how each discovery could be applied by others, advancing understanding of the world's natural forces. Faraday's experiments went on to create the first transformer as he connected one charged iron ring, encircled by a coil of wire attached to a battery, with a second coil wrapped around a different portion of the iron ring and attached to a galvanometer. The magnetic field generated by the first coil set up a current in the second coil, as recorded by the galvanometer.

Faraday's lectures throughout Europe became increasingly popular. During one lecture, he demonstrated the lines of force generated by a magnet

English chemist and physicist Michael Faraday discovered electromagnetism, the manipulation of magnetism to make electricity, using an experiment similar to the one shown here.

by inserting a magnet into a coil of wire attached to a galvanometer. During the process, as the magnet was being positioned, current flowed through the wire. When the magnet was held stationary and the coil moved over it, there was current found in the wire. If both were held motionless, no current appeared. Remarkably, onstage in 1831, Faraday discovered electrical induction—also independently found by Joseph Henry in America that same year.

ELECTRIC CURRENTS

Since electricity seemed to vary in intensity and strength, German physicist Georg Simon Ohm (1789–1854) decided to use his master mechanic's skills to design wires of different widths and test the electric current. Ohm was building on the work of Jean Baptiste Joseph Fourier (1768–1830), a French scholar who wrote *The Analytic Theory of Heat*, the first study of the way heat moved between objects. This work led to the famous Fourier theorem, which states that any periodic variation, however complex, can be broken into a series of simple regular wave motions, the sum of which will be the original complex periodic variation.

Ohm's results were refined into what is known today as Ohm's law: the flow of current through a conductor is directly proportional to the potential difference and inversely proportional to the resistance. (It should be noted that England's Henry Cavendish came to the same conclusion fifty years earlier, but since he never published the work, it was not then known.) At the time, Ohm's work and methodology received harsh criticism since much of it was theoretical. Over time, though, his work gained acceptance, and the unit used to measure resistance is now known as the ohm.

In summary, when one ampere passes through a substance under a potential difference of one volt, that substance has a resistance of one ohm. Lord Kelvin went on to whimsically name the unit of conductance (the opposite of resistance) the mho.

In 1831, this new knowledge would find its way out of the lab with Faraday's electric generator, developed after his experimentation with inducing electric energy in a continuous fashion. Prior to that moment, the only way to obtain electricity was through a chemical battery. By using a steam engine, Faraday could turn a copper wheel so that its edge passed between the poles of a permanently affixed magnet. When a current was passed through the copper wheel, it continued as long as the wheel spun. This excess energy could then be drawn off and, like the steam engine itself, be put to work.

JOSEPH HENRY

All the research and discovery was not limited to Europe. Joseph Henry (1797–1878) was the first major American scientist to follow after Benjamin Franklin. Henry was aware of Sturgeon using Ørsted's research to form the electromagnet. Henry wanted to build something stronger but knew that simply using more wires wrapped around a coil would cause short circuits. He then conceived the idea of finding an insulating material that would prevent short circuits without interfering with the charge. He began by using his wife's silk petticoats and continued to experiment. This insulation,

the result of countless hours spent wrapping individual wires, proved effective, resulting in greater attraction. By 1831, Henry had developed an electromagnet powerful enough to pull 750 pounds (340 kg), more than 83 times the pull of Sturgeon's first device. Within a year, one of his magnets had pulled a ton of weight.

In addition to huge magnets, Henry also developed a series of smaller, more intimate magnets for finer work. He was working with the notion of creating a circuit that would send the magnetic pull through a wire and attract something a long distance away. His work challenged Ohm's law regarding the resistance and smaller current in relation to distance. Henry developed an electrical relay in 1835, managing a current to attract an iron key, activating the relay. A series of such relays allowed power to flow over much greater distances. The switching on and off of the key controlled the flow of power. In effect, Henry developed the principles for the first telegraph. Henry unselfishly shared his findings, which were then seized by Samuel Morse, who improved upon them and patented them himself. Meanwhile, Henry also advised Sir Charles Wheatstone, allowing

Samuel Morse used the concept of Joseph Henry's findings in electricity to develop the telegraph, the first means of transmitting messages over a long distance.

the Englishman to set up Europe's first telegraph line in 1837. Today, Henry's work has been recognized, but at the time, neither Morse nor Wheatstone publicly acknowledged his contributions.

Henry did, however, gain credit for the notion of self-induction: an electric current in a coil can induce another current not only in another coil but also in itself. This means the current in a coil is actually the original current and the induced current.

Henry published a scientific paper in 1831 that reversed the idea of the electric generator and was the first to conceive of the electric motor. Mechanical force is employed to generate the current in the former, while Henry described the current creating the mechanical force in the latter. Therefore, Faraday's work led Henry to postulate a device to employ the generator. The revolutionary ideas took time to catch on and be put to practical use.

If Henry was disappointed to be second to Faraday, imagine being third. The Russian physicist Heinrich Friedrich Emil Lenz (1804–1865) also came up with the theory of electrical induction but published after the others. Still, in 1834, Lenz did conceive the law that a current induced by electromagnetic forces always produces effects that oppose those forces. Today, Lenz's law is considered one of the important laws needed to design electrical equipment.

MEASURING HEAT

Along with the generating of electric current came the generating of heat, yet this was initially over-looked. The first to pay attention to this was James Prescott Joule (1818–1889), who started measuring heat. Joule was fascinated with measurements of all kinds and was drawn to the heat given off by electricity. Before he was twenty, Joule had already written several papers on the measurement of heat. By 1840, Joule had come up with a formula to exactly measure the heat produced by an electric current. The heat generated is proportional to the square of the current's intensity multiplied by the resistance of the circuit.

For the next decade, Joule passed electric currents through every substance imaginable, measuring the heat along the way. He noted how the level of heat rose or fell whether water flowed over a paddle or gases expanded. This led to reasoning that built off the work, a century earlier, of Benjamin Thompson, Count Rumford. Count Rumford (1753–1814) is not only noted for introducing the steam engine and the potato to the European continent, but for develop-ing the theory that mechanical motion generated heat, making heat a by-product of motion and not a separate substance. He was also the first to attempt to measure heat, and his standards remained until corrected by Joule.

Joule compressed air and measured the heat created, followed by agitating water with a paddle. He then tried this with a series of other liquids and his resulting measures led to his value of 772 foot-pounds as the amount of work needed to raise the temperature of a pound of water by 1° Fahrenheit. This became known as the British thermal unit, or BTU. He found that a set quantity of work produced a fixed amount of heat, known today as the mechanical equivalent of heat.

At first, his conclusions were met with disdain from the scientific community, either because he was not a professor or because the measurements were too minute to concern the other scientists. In that time, there was little attention paid to those without credentials in their fields. Joule was a child of wealth and was indulged in his studies but never taught. Instead, when his father died, he took over running the family brewery, but he never once stopped indulging his studies. He, like Davy and Faraday, turned to the public and gave lectures and then had them published in the local newspaper. It wasn't until 1849 that Joule's work was accepted. This came when Faraday sponsored a lecture by him at the Royal Society.

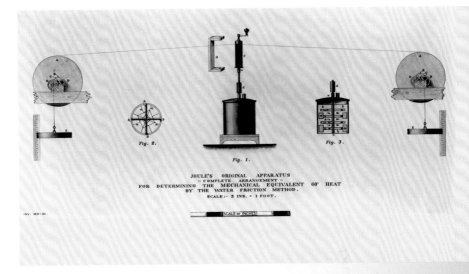

James Prescott Joule's apparatus was the first of its kind for determining the mechanical equivalent of heat. The units of measurement would eventually come to bear his name.

Joule's studies showed that energy changes in several ways, not just between the measures of kinetic and potential energy. Some of that energy is changed to heat, which was now being measured and considered for the first time. Today, a joule has become a measure for work: 10,000,000 ergs is a joule; 4.18 joules equals 1 calorie of heat.

Joule's measurements led to the law of conservation of energy, which states that energy can neither be created out of nothing nor destroyed into nothing, but can only be changed from one form to another. This law would coincide with important studies in thermodynamics that were being conducted in France by Sadi Carnot (1796–1832). First, Carnot studied the heat given off by Watt's steam engine. The measure of this engine's efficiency was under 10 percent. Carnot was curious about the remaining 90-plus percent. He measured the cold water versus the point of steam emission, the two temperature extremes. His equation for the maximum fraction for heat energy that could be converted to work energy was:

$$\frac{T1 - T2}{T2}$$

Unfortunately, his work went mainly unnoticed until nearly two decades after his death.

POWERING THE INDUSTRIAL REVOLUTION

Chapter

4

J oule was not alone in his studies of the conservation of energy. Today, he shares the credit for this theory with two German scientists, Hermann Ludwig Helmholtz (1821–1894) and Julius Robert Mayer (1814–1878). Helmholtz was measuring the speed of nerve impulses when he was led to study energy itself. While Mayer announced the theory first, in 1842, Helmholtz provided far greater detail five years later. Helmholtz began studying the way animals reacted to stimulus and wanted to prove the "vitalists"—those who thought all animals had some innate vital force—wrong.

He studied the animals and then energy itself, concluding that if they had a vital source independent of chemical interactions, they would run with inexhaustible energy and be living perpetual motion machines, which clearly animals were not. He concluded animal heat and muscle action were generated by changes in the muscles. From this conclusion, he refined the notion of energy being converted from one form of matter to another. He had difficulty getting his idea published and did so in a self-published pamphlet.

Julius Robert Mayer presented his notion for the mechanical equivalent of heat in 1842, but like Helmholtz, he was delayed in publishing. Mayer used a horse to power a device that stirred paper pulp. When he compared the horse's efforts with the rise in pulp temperature, he was able to devise a mathematical formula. It was a crude conclusion, and when he published it, it was largely ignored until Joule refined the notion on his own. While Helmholtz was more precise in his mathematics, Mayer was broader in his studies, deriving the

The German scientist Julius Robert Mayer was one of the first to study how the muscle action of animals was the result of one form of energy being converted to another.

mechanical conversion of energy to other phenomena, such as the tides. Like Helmholtz, he saw no extraordinary power source in animals. This was an alarming notion in an era when most scientists felt that the laws applied to animate objects were different than the laws applied to inanimate objects. Mayer went so far as to suggest that solar power provided the energy for all things—both living and nonliving—on Earth.

Mayer was initially ignored or scorned, but first Joule then others began to speak approvingly of his methods and conclusions. Despite a failed suicide attempt and other personal tragedies, Mayer was finally acknowledged, receiving accolades and awards for his life's work.

Lord Kelvin

During this time of great scientific advancement, it became the responsibility of a few innovators to galvanize the public's imagination. One way they achieved this was by providing demonstrations of their experiments on stage. They made the general public aware of new discoveries and theories, which proved inspirational for some who followed in the speaker's footsteps. Some scientists took the opportunity to speak out on behalf of their ignored peers. One such person, speaking in favor of Joule's beliefs, was William Thomson (1824–1907), who, after being knighted, became Lord Kelvin. A contemporary of Joule's and Helmholtz's during this exciting time of discovery, he helped to advance the theories on energy. Thomson himself was a brilliant mathematician, entering the University of Glasgow at age eleven.

As a young professor, Thomson had been fascinated by the studies on heat and the works of Joule. The two eventually collaborated, resulting in the realization that gases dropped in temperature as they expanded in a vacuum. In actuality, Thomson is better known for his work with the absence of heat. In 1848, he presented the theory that the energy of a gas's molecular motion reached zero at -459° Fahrenheit (-273° Celsius). This was a new demarcation for absolute zero and the resulting scale was later named the Kelvin scale in his honor.

The Kelvin scale proved essential in corroborating the work of other scientists, such as Carnot. He had stated that the maximum work derived from a heat engine relied on temperature differences within the engine itself. Now this could be expressed mathematically by employing the Kelvin scale.

One of the devices Lord Kelvin invented was called the harmonic analyzer, which recorded the daily changes in atmospheric temperature and pressure.

Building off Carnot's work, Thomson determined that all energy dissipates as heat. The 1851 idea of "degradation," a term given to the loss of heat in all things from the sun to a cooling tea, was entirely new, as was the extension of that thinking—that the entire universe was "winding down." It was from these studies that the idea of entropy would begin. Entropy is a way to measure the spread of a given form of energy. It would be decades before this was applied entirely to the universe in the second law of thermodynamics.

Thomson also devoted himself to studying the amount of current that could be successfully sent through a cable. This was of great help to Cyrus Field, who in 1866 was laying a cable across the Atlantic Ocean, attempting to connect England to America. It was Field who introduced Alexander Graham Bell's telephone to England.

While Thomson devoted himself to practical matters, Rudolf Julius Emanuel Clausius (1822–1888) was more a theoretician. For example, he was the first to propose theories regarding what would happen when electricity was passed through solutions, suggesting the molecules might be pulled apart. But he did not go into the laboratory to prove himself correct. He left that for others. Still, his theory of "dissociation" was proven accurate.

Today, Clausius is best known for corroborating the work of Carnot and Thomson concerning the degradation of energy. The ratio of the heat content of a system and its absolute temperature, found by using the Kelvin scale, would always increase in any process occurring in a closed system—a system that neither gains nor loses energy to the outside world. The universe is the only known closed system. Taking this to an extreme gave birth to Clausius's "heat death" of the universe theory, which saw that equilibrium could be generated between heat extremes, and with nothing left to flow, the universe would come to a conclusion.

In a perfect closed system, the ratio would remain constant. Instead, this heat event always increases, never the opposite. This theory was compatible with Thomson's theory, and since they were proposed simultaneously, the scientific community took notice.

His theory of entropy was presented in 1850. Clausius explained that as entropy occurred, there was less energy to work with; the more entropy—such as heat escaping from an object—the less matter to turn into usable energy. For this discovery, Clausius is credited as the author of the second law of thermodynamics.

MEASURING LIGHT

While some scientists applied these conclusions to chemistry, others were increasingly fascinated with light and its properties. Helmholtz's work in this area proved inspirational to his assistant, Wilhelm Wien (1864–1928), who took it even further. Not only did the amount of radiation from light fascinate him, but so did light's very nature. Helmholtz and Wien created what they would call a black

body—an enclosed, heated black box, with a tiny hole. Wien defined this as an ideal body, which completely absorbs all radiation. The hole allowed light into the box where it was trapped. The blackness within should absorb the light and emit radiation on all wavelengths. Wien measured what was actually emitted and applied the known thermodynamic theories to the wavelengths. In 1893, he wrote how the radiation peaked at a point that was inverse to the temperature. He concluded that as the temperature rose, the predominant color shifts toward the blue end of the color spectrum. Hotter, though, and the shift moved to the red end, emitting light first seen as red and gradually gaining brilliance to yellow-white and finally blue-white. This effect can be seen when a log fire is built: as the wood burns generating heat, the light also changes in hue as the fire grows hotter.

Wien was frustrated when he could not formulate an equation that would allow light to be expressed in all wavelengths when radiation is emitted from the black body. Only a short range of radiation worked

Wilhelm Wien won the 1911 Nobel Prize in Physics for his work on radiation of heat from the black body, which paved the way for future advancements in quantum physics.

under his theory. Like many of his contemporaries, Wien was determined to find a formula that encompassed the totality of his subject. Other scientists had managed to formulate equations for one end of the light spectrum or another, but not the whole. However, one scientists was about to rewrite the rules of physics.

INTRODUCING STANDARD MEASUREMENTS

Scientists were continually hampered by the lack of standard measurements. With the rapid growth of science in the eighteenth century, the need for a standard measure for dimensions became paramount. When Charles-Marie de La Condamine (1701–1774) was exploring South America—part of a grand quest to help measure the exact size and shape of Earth—he sent back his topographic and cartography studies, but there was no European agreement for height, weight, or length. As a result, his results were at variance with his colleagues Pierre Louis Maupertuis, Pierre Bouguer, and Alexis Claude

Clairaut. Upon his return, he was one of the most vocal proponents for a standard system.

He died in 1774, nearly two decades before the metric system was adopted in the 1790s. Platinum, given its weight and durability, was used to create the standards for the meter and the kilogram, adopted on June 22, 1799. These were the first two steps in the development of the International System of Units.

Not every nation accepted this at first. It took until 1832 before astronomical standards were adopted to help describe and define the universe, unifying various branches of science. The British Association for the Advancement of Science (BAAS) was formed in 1831, and by the 1860s, standards for measuring electricity and magnetism were adopted.

In 1874, the BAAS introduced a three-dimensional coherent unit system based on the three mechanical units: centimeter, gram, and second. By the 1880s, the BAAS and the International Electrical Congress developed a new set of standards including the ohm, volt, and ampere.

Over the years, unified scientific bodies have met and refined or adopted new standards. The United States developed its own system of weights and measures. In the 1970s, the United States began using metric measures along with the American system, with the intent of one day converting entirely to the metric system to match most of the world. At the dawn of the twenty-first century, that conversion has yet to be complete.

Max Planck was instrumental in the advancement of the study of the nature of energy. His developments led to some of the most ground-breaking work in quantum physics.

Max Karl Ernst Ludwig Planck (1858–1947), who also studied under Helmholtz in Germany, restated Clausius's law, saying, "It is impossible to construct an engine which, working in a complete cycle, will produce no effect other than the raising of a weight and the cooling of a heat reservoir."

Planck, though, is known today for his brilliant theory that led to a new era for physicists. In addition to his research into heat dissipation, or entropy, he was a keen observer of light. He spent years trying to find a mathematical formula that could explain why a black body could absorb all frequencies of light but, when heated, emit radiation at a limited number of frequencies. Much of this had to do with the notion that there are many more frequencies at

the higher end of the scale than the lower, just as there are more numbers over 1,000,000 than under.

As the century turned, in 1900, Planck put forth an equation that contained a startling assumption: energy, like matter, is contained in particles and is therefore not infinitely divisible. These packets of energy were named quanta (Latin for "how much").

Planck's introduction of quantum theory changed the way scientists looked at the world's matter and is considered the dividing line between "classic physics" and "modern physics."

ENERGY IN THE MODERN WORLD

Chapter 5

While many scientists were drawn to these new groundbreaking theories, others continued to refine what is now considered classic physics. With the Industrial Revolution in full swing throughout the nineteenth century, machines became more efficient; steam power allowed boats to travel faster and gave rise to locomotives. A vast, far-reaching world suddenly seemed much smaller and accessible as goods traveled from country to country in weeks rather than months.

This also altered the way people lived. Machines replaced some unskilled labor, giving rise to those who built and maintained the machines. The need for child labor was reduced, improving life at home.

Ushering in a new age, Thomas Alva Edison put the past discoveries in energy to a very practical use—the lightbulb—which revolutionized the way humankind worked and lived.

Telegraphs allowed news to spread in a far timelier manner, making the general public better informed.

THE LIGHTBULB

The prodigious efforts of Thomas Alva Edison (1847–1931), though, would have the greatest impact on the modern, practical use of energy. Edison was a self-made man, overcoming his childhood deafness to learn and prosper. After young Edison rescued a small boy from the train tracks, the grateful father of the child taught Edison telegraphy and Edison quickly became the speediest and best operator in America.

Edison's first invention he planned to sell was a machine that tabulated votes faster. However, politicians rejected it in favor of the slow process of voting.

His next invention, the stock ticker, came from his experience at a New York City brokerage. Edison planned to ask $5,000 for the device, but instead the company president offered the twenty-three-year-old $40,000.

Moving his home to Menlo Park, New Jersey, Edison employed a group of assistants and set out to invent something new every ten days. By his death, he had 1,300 patents for such devices. The press dubbed him the Wizard of Menlo Park, a name he quite liked.

Edison was determined to find a practical way to make light from electricity, which by that time had been freely flowing around the United States. It was a daunting task, as several scientists before him had attempted and failed. Edison knew it required electricity heating a wire and that the wire had to be contained in a vacuum. Edison spent over a year searching for the right filament to use that could handle the sustained heat. He thought platinum was the answer, but after investing $50,000, he was proven wrong. No metal could handle such power without melting. The solution presented itself in the form of nothing metallic, but a simple cotton thread. Such a bulb was ignited on October 21, 1879, and it burned for forty consecutive hours. Edison had his answer.

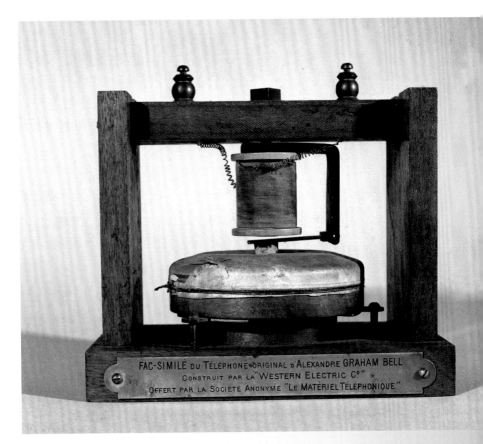

FAC-SIMILÉ DU TÉLÉPHONE ORIGINAL D'ALEXANDRE GRAHAM BELL
CONSTRUIT PAR LA "WESTERN ELECTRIC C°"
OFFERT PAR LA SOCIÉTÉ ANONYME "LE MATÉRIEL TÉLÉPHONIQUE"

Other technologies that utilized the harnessing of energy include the telephone. There's debate about who invented the telephone even though Alexander Graham Bell received the patent.

The next challenge was to find a way to produce an electric current that the consumer could easily switch on and off, making the lightbulb practical. In time, Edison built such a generating system and powered eighty-five customers with 400 outlets in 1881. Edison's power was applying direct current, which ultimately proved less efficient to generate and transmit than alternating current.

Among Edison's numerous inventions are everyday items such as wax paper and the phonograph. He also refined the telephone mouthpiece, the work of his contemporary, Alexander Graham Bell, making the overall device practical for a mass populace. Bell returned the favor years later by improving on the phonograph. Bell (1847–1922) was an inventor who first wanted to improve on the telegraph. Bell used theories dating back to Helmholtz to develop the first practical use of telephonic communication.

AC/DC

The new powerful world of business brought about by the Industrial Revolution not only changed commerce but also created secure environments for scientists to flourish in their research of the developing world of electricity. Charles Proteus Steinmetz (1865–1923) was one such brilliant scientist who benefited from General Electric absorbing the small factory where he worked. Born in Germany, he fled the persecution he experienced there for being Jewish and hunchback, even changing his birth name Karl for a more

"American" name. His greatest achievement is said to be the use of complex variable mathematics to develop design equations for alternating current devices. Steinmetz's equations enabled the design of very efficient alternating current (AC) motors that were more efficient than motors using a different charge known as direct current (DC). He then built intricate equipment to generate high output electricity and held over 200 patents.

Steinmetz's work was a boon to Nikola Tesla (1856–1943), the great Croatian inventor. He studied engineering in Europe, but soon after he came to America and initially worked for Thomas Edison. They had a falling out over money, and Tesla went his own way. He concentrated, at first, on developing ways to transmit electricity through cables so as to minimize energy loss over great distances. He developed a better class of transformer that would change low voltage electricity to a higher voltage for better transmission and then reduce the voltage at its destination. Direct current involved a constant current flowing in one direction in the circuit whereas alternating current changed polarity from positive to negative, frequently in the same circuit, which provided a stronger charge.

These transformers worked best with alternating current, which put Tesla at further opposition with

ABLE EXTRAIT DE VIANDE LIEBIG.

L'ÉLECTRICITÉ.

avec son transformateur produisant la lumière au moyen de l'électricité

Nikola Tesla is known for his developments in electromagnetism in the late nineteenth and early twentieth centuries. In this illustration, he demonstrates his transformer, which produces light by means of electricity.

with Edison. While Tesla developed motors that could use the newly delivered AC power, Edison lobbied vigorously for direct current to be the standard in America, starting with New York State. Edison was passionate about this since it further enhanced his control over technological improvements across America, not to mention endless revenues.

Tesla allied himself with Edison's competitor George Westinghouse (1846–1914). Westinghouse, who introduced the air brake to trains in 1868, took the work of early physicists to heart. Compressed air proved more powerful than human muscles, and the air brake improved the performance of trains, conserving energy from the crew and the wear and tear on the equipment itself.

Westinghouse found Tesla's work with alternating current fascinating and together they proved the greater efficiency in transporting AC power throughout the country. Edison's direct current was ultimately thwarted, especially when Westinghouse received the contract to harness Niagara Falls' hydro energy to generate AC power.

With electricity now flowing through high-tension wires strung between generators and buildings, cities lit up at night, and factories could work around the clock without the noxious fumes from kerosene lanterns or exposed gaslights. Society was forever changed by the lightbulb.

ON THE SUBATOMIC LEVEL

One of Edison's inventions would be slightly ahead of its time. He enclosed a piece of metal within a lightbulb and watched in fascination as the electricity in the filament was transmitted through the vacuum to the metal. Although he patented this development, he found no practical application for it.

The ways in which humankind has harnessed energy, such as the invention of the lightbulb, have changed the way we work, play, and live.

Then, Sir Joseph John Thomson (1856–1940) wanted to build upon James Clerk Maxwell's (1831–1879) work with electromagnetic radiation. He was the mathematician who turned Faraday's theories of magnetic lines of force into actual equations. Cathode rays, emitted from light, were believed to be non-electromagnetic and to contain negatively charged particles. No conclusive proof existed until Thomson began working with the rays and vacuum tubes.

In 1897, these rays were deflected in an electric field, providing the final piece to the puzzle. When he studied the ratio of the ray's particulate charge to its mass, applying Faraday's laws of electrochemistry, he noted that the mass was only a fraction of hydrogen atoms. That made the ray particles smaller than atoms and thus the field of subatomic particles was born. These cathode ray particles were named, over Thomson's objection, electrons following a theory proposed years before by George Johnstone Stoney (1826–1911). Stoney was the physicist who first postulated that electricity was not a fluid but instead a flow of particles. Still, Thomson used the electron to begin theorizing upon the makeup of the atom itself.

Sir John Ambrose Fleming (1849–1945) was able to take this further. The son of a congregational minister, he had the advantage of being exposed to Edison's unused discovery. At the time of that discovery, Fleming had consulted with Edison as the electric light industry was brought to England in the 1880s. Fleming also had the benefit of having worked with Guglielmo Marchese Marconi (1874–1937), the father of the radio, and he combined the lessons from both men.

The leap of electricity from the hot filament to the cold metal wire within the lightbulb was actually the newly discovered electrons being cast off the hot filament. Fleming learned this only occurred when the metal wire was attached to a generator's positive terminal and it attracted the oppositely charged electrons. When using alternating current, Fleming learned that only

In 1896, Joseph John Thomson began experiments on cathode rays. Thomson used this device to show that the cathode rays were particles with a negative charge and much smaller than an atom.

half the alternating current would move through the wire, so alternating current entered, but direct current, the singularly charged form of electricity, would exit.

What we've learned over the past several thousand years about the nature of energy can be put to a range of uses, from shifting the course of humankind to changing the way we spend our leisure time.

Fleming called this newly developed device a rectifier, but in the United States, it was called a tube. Later, the tube, the cathode ray, and electricity would be further combined in unique ways to bring about the first radio, followed by the television.

The Future of Energy

As a result of Edison's, Tesla's, Westinghouse's, and others' efforts to bring about commercial uses of energy, the benefits of "classic physics" became readily apparent to every man and woman around the world. Their work brought about improvements in the daily life of millions.

Also, as cheap electricity became plentiful, factories refined their practices and manufacturing boomed.

One practical change came about when Henry Ford introduced the assembly line to factory work. Suddenly products could be built with greater speed. Ford benefited from this with the rapid production of automobiles, and the assembly line was quickly adopted throughout America and Europe.

It was in that environment, at the turn of the twentieth century, that some of the greatest mathematical thinking occurred. Based on the findings of Max Planck, these new theories would change the concept of energy and the world in many ways.

EINSTEIN'S THEORIES

Albert Einstein (1879–1955), the German-born mathematician, had been an average if not poor student during his early years. However, equations he doodled during his idle time while working in a Swiss patent office led to the publishing of five papers in 1905's *German Yearbook of Physics*.

In his first paper, Einstein examined how light falling on certain metals stimulated the emission of electrons, known today as the photoelectric effect. Here, Einstein used Planck's then-new quantum theory to help explain why a brighter light did not produce more energetic electrons. The wavelength of light would cause only a fixed electron to be emitted from the metal. Einstein determined that the wavelength of light after fixed points produced differing forms of electron activity.

His second paper, published two months later, was in an entirely different field. Here, he developed a mathematical reasoning for Brownian motion, named after botanist Robert Brown (1773–1858) for his discovery of the erratic motion of particles when viewed under a microscope. He determined how and why particles, such as dust, in liquid moved when struck by randomly moving molecules from a gas. The major significance of this paper was that the size of molecules could not be determined through math. This led to the development of measuring atom size.

The third paper, however, is the one for which Einstein is best remembered. He claimed he developed a formula to explain the lack of symmetry in Maxwell's work on electromagnetic effects. Did the velocity of light and change in direction or substance the light moved through have any effect on speed? Einstein, measuring light in quanta particles, said no. Years later, the particle of light was named the photon by Arthur Compton.

Einstein further theorized that nothing in the universe was at absolute rest or absolute motion, but

that everything worked in relation to one another. With all things being relative to one another, Einstein developed the world-renowned theory of relativity: $E = mc^2$. E is energy, m is mass, and c is the velocity of light. By separating these different aspects of the same phenomena, Einstein's equation had joined space and time together in what is known as the space-time continuum.

In 1915, Einstein managed to publish a paper of even greater significance, replacing Newton's theory of gravity: the force of attraction between two bodies is proportional to the product of their masses and inversely proportional to the square of the distance between them. More accurately, Einstein made Newton's theory a subset of a general theory of relativity. Broken into three components, Einstein's general theory helped better define and measure the universe. One component accounted for the shift of a planet's perihelion, or point at which it is closest to the sun, such as takes place in Mercury's orbit. This covered a phenomenon that Newton's work did not allow for. The second component allowed for light, caught in an intense gravitational field, such as that

Albert Einstein, along with Isaac Newton, is considered one of the greatest minds in science. His findings on the relationship between mass and energy changed the way we view the nature of energy.

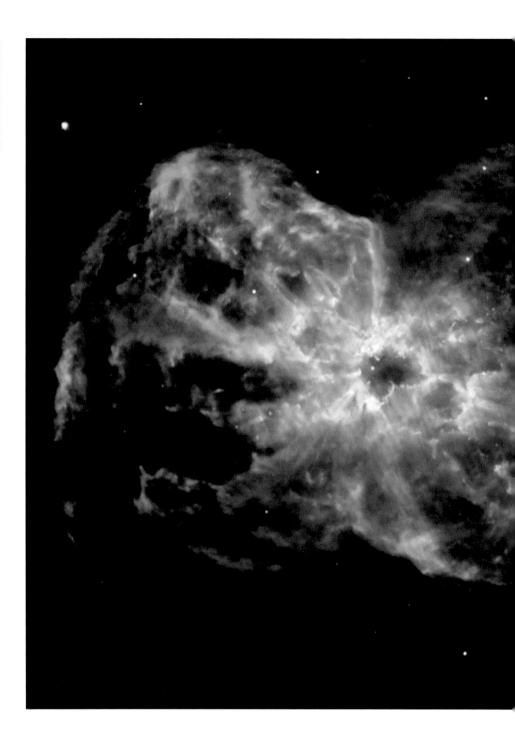

Today, we have the ability to study the heavens like never before. By analyzing celestial phenomena, such as the death of stars, we can study the nature of energy in new ways.

of a white dwarf star, to show a red shift—a shift in the spectra of distant galaxies toward longer wavelengths.

In relation to the second component, the third allowed for light to be deflected by a gravitational field, something he managed to prove on March 29, 1919, during a solar eclipse, when measurements of bright stars were taken in the Gulf of Guinea and Brazil.

Einstein's work made him famous, perhaps the most world-famous scientist since Newton himself. He was lecturing in America when Adolf Hitler took power in Germany, so he stayed and accepted a position at Princeton University. In 1940, before America's entry into World War II, Einstein became an American citizen. Einstein wrote to President Franklin Delano Roosevelt, advocating that America develop the

On a cautionary note, our understanding of how energy works enabled us to build nuclear weapons, which have the potential to literally destroy humankind.

atomic bomb. Once he became aware of uranium fission in 1939, it was only a matter of time before someone learned how to harness that energy in a destructive manner. Better, the great scientist thought, that America find that method before Hitler's own researchers did.

The top secret Manhattan Project exploded the first such device on July 16, 1945, months after Roosevelt died and after Hitler had been defeated. Weeks later, the only two atomic bombs built were deployed over Japan, bringing an end to World War II. Its horrific effects on the people and the land stood as a testament to the destructive forces now in man's control.

In Einstein's waning years, he was a vocal advocate for a worldwide ban on such devastating weapons.

5 SEC.

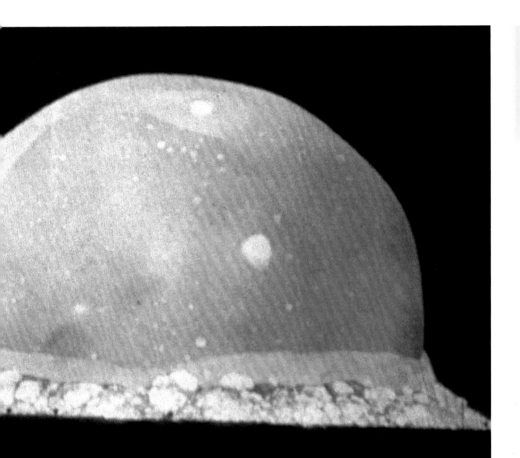

100 METERS

Instead, more countries developed their own atomic bombs, a trend that continues to this day. However, harnessing the power of the atom also allowed for nuclear plants generating power for millions.

YESTERDAY, TODAY, AND TOMORROW

Since Einstein's theories a century ago, the world has undergone dramatic changes. By mastering electricity and magnetism, learning how to conserve energy, how to channel its changing forms to get more productivity out of mechanical energy, and then understanding matter down to the subatomic level, we have changed everything about the way we live and work.

Without these discoveries, the Industrial Revolution would not have been possible. Without all the subsequent work, we would not enjoy simple electric lights or the wonders of the Internet or benefit from learning about our universe through the space probes launched from our own shores.

Many of the most fundamental discoveries about the nature of energy and how it works in our universe have been recorded over the last five centuries. The work of countless scientists and physicists today all build upon the work of these largely self-taught pioneers. Einstein's work has been refined but not replaced.

GREEN ENERGY IN BLOOM

Green energy, or energy that's environmentally friendly, is the future of the industry. There are many "sustainable" forms of energy being developed and enhanced, including wind, geothermal, and ocean energy, to name just a few. There are also highly innovative alternatives such as the Bloom Box, produced by a company called Bloom Energy. Also called the Bloom Energy Saver, the device is a solid oxide fuel cell (SOFC), first built in the 1950s, that generates electricity on site from available resources such as liquid or hydrocarbons. The company claims that the Bloom Box is at least as efficient as large-scale coal power stations.

While the first SOFC was built in the 1950s, the current Bloom Box is designed for common consumption in homes and businesses. Oxygen is fed into one side of the device while fuel in any number of forms is supplied to the other side. The result is a chemical reaction that produces power.

K. R. Sridhar, founder of Bloom Energy, claims that two Bloom Boxes, each roughly the size of a shoebox, can power the average high-consumption American home. Larger-scale devices can power entire businesses. In fact, major companies such as FedEx, Wal-Mart, eBay, and Google have already begun using them, offering hope for true energy independence.

In his lifetime, Einstein did not find a formula, equation, or even a theory to unify time, space, light, and matter. This remains the ultimate quest for physicists today, and most likely tomorrow. With every discovery and theory, whether it is the idea of super strings in space or the existence of the muon (an elementary particle with a negative charge), we come closer to understanding the physical makeup of matter and the universe. While it's doubtful that any one discovery will change society as it has in the past, our knowledge of the universe will vastly improve.

25,000 years ago Early man starts regularly using wood for fire during the Stone Age.

3000 BCE Man first harnesses wind energy in the form of sailboats.

1000 BCE The Chinese are the first to use coal to smelt copper.

624 BCE Thales of Miletus is born. He is the first to attempt to explain the nature of energy rather than trying to ascribe the acts to the gods.

570 BCE Anaximenes is born. He is the first to declare that air was the principal element in the universe.

540 BCE Heraclitus of Ephesus is born. He is the first to declare that fire was the primal element, which ruled the world.

490 BCE Empedocles of Agrigentum is born. He is the first to conclude that the universe is made up of the four elements: water, air, fire, and earth.

800 CE Muslims first utilize windmills to turn large stones to grind grains.

1712 The Miner's Friend, the first practical water pump, is invented, proving the ability to convert one form of energy to another.

1746 The Leiden jar, the first device to store electricity, is invented.

1752 Benjamin Franklin conducts his famous electric kite experiment.

1761 Scottish chemist Joseph Black helps determine how much energy exists when water is turned to steam.

1765 James Watt revolutionizes the steam engine, which contributes to the Industrial Revolution.

1807 Sir Humphry Davy succeeds in extracting a substance from potash, which he names potassium.

1831 Michael Faraday discovers electrical induction.

1840 James Prescott Joule discovers a formula to exactly measure the heat produced by an electric current.

1879 The lightbulb is invented by Thomas Alva Edison.

1900 Max Planck develops the quantum theory.

1905 Albert Einstein develops his theory of special relativity, which partly states that mass and energy are related.

2010 Photovoltaics, an energy technology that converts solar radiation into electricity using semiconductors, generates electricity in more than 100 countries and is the fastest-growing energy technology in the world.

acceleration The rate of change of velocity over time.

conservation of energy The principle in physics that states that the total energy of an isolated system remains constant.

energy The entity of nature that creates change. The two most important forms are kinetic energy and potential energy. In the absence of external forces such as air resistance and friction, the total amount of an object's energy remains constant.

force A degree of energy that is expressed over a certain distance and time.

friction A force that resists the motion of an object. Friction results from the close interaction between two surfaces that are sliding across each other.

gravity The fundamental force that is responsible for the attraction of any bodies that have mass.

horsepower A unit of power equal to 746 watts.

hybrid The combination of two or more elements.

Industrial Revolution The economic revolution that took place in the West during the end of the eighteenth century, which shifted manufacturing from being home based and small to large scale.

inertia The tendency of an object to resist change in its state of motion.

kinetic energy The energy possessed by an object because of its motion, which depends upon the mass and speed of the object.

law of interaction Newton's third law of motion, which states that for every action, there is an equal and opposite reaction.

mass The measurement of the amount of material in a substance; the quantity of matter.

perihelion The point in the course of a planet's orbit when it's closest to the sun.

potential energy The energy possessed by an object.

Renaissance The period of artistic, scientific, philosophical, and cultural blossoming that began in the fourteenth century in Italy and lasted into the seventeenth century.

speed A measurement of how fast an object is moving.

watt A unit of power equal to the work done at the rate of one joule per second.

weight A measurement of the gravitational force acting on an object.

For More Information

Bloom Energy
1252 Orleans Drive
Sunnyvale, CA 94089
(408) 543-1500
Web site: http://www.bloomenergy.com
Bloom Energy is a cutting-edge energy technology company
that produces the Bloom Box.

Energy Council of Canada
350 Sparks Street
Suite 608
Ottawa, ON K1R 7S8
Canada
(613) 232-8239
Web site: http://www.energy.ca
The Energy Council of Canada oversees the policies of Canada's
energy resources and usage.

Energy Kids
U.S. Department of Energy
Energy Information Administration (EI-30)
1000 Independence Avenue SW
Washington, DC 20585
(202) 586-8800
Web site: http://www.eia.doe.gov/kids
This kid-friendly Web site of the U.S. Department of Energy
explains what energy is and how it's used.

U.S. Department of Energy
1000 Independence Avenue SW
Washington, DC 20585
(202) 586-5000
Web site: http://www.energy.gov
The U.S. Department of Energy is the cabinet-level department of the U.S. government responsible for the nation's energy policies.

Web Sites

Due to the changing nature of Internet links, Rosen Publishing has developed an online list of Web sites related to the subject of this book. This site is updated regularly. Please use this link to access the list:

http://www.rosenlinks.com/phys/ener

Bauman, Amy. *Earth's Natural Resources*. Strongsville, OH: Gareth Stevens Publishing, 2008.

Brezina, Corona. *Climate Change*. New York, NY: Rosen Publishing Group, 2007.

Crosby, Alfred W. *Children of the Sun: A History of Humanity's Unappeasable Appetite for Energy*. New York, NY: W. W. Norton & Company, 2006.

Friedman, Thomas L. *Hot, Flat, and Crowded 2.0: Why We Need a Green Revolution—and How It Can Renew America*. New York, NY: Picador, 2009.

Gleick, James. *Isaac Newton*. New York, NY: Vintage, 2004.

Isaacson, Walter. *Benjamin Franklin: An American Life*. New York, NY: Simon & Schuster, 2004.

Kaku, Michio. *Physics of the Impossible: A Scientific Exploration into the World of Phasers, Force Fields, Teleportation, and Time Travel*. New York, NY: Anchor, 2009.

Lindley, David. *Degrees Kelvin: A Tale of Genius, Invention, and Tragedy*. Washington, DC: Joseph Henry Press, 2005.

Passero, Barbara, ed. *Energy Alternatives: Opposing Viewpoints*. Farmington Hills, MI: Greenhaven Press, 2006.

Rae, Alastair I. M. *Quantum Physics: A Beginner's Guide*. Oxford, England: Oneworld Publications, 2006.

Raum, Elizabeth. *Potato Clocks and Solar Cars: Renewable and Non-renewable Energy*. Chicago, IL: Heinemann-Raintree, 2007.

Rosenblum, Bruce. *Quantum Enigma: Physics Encounters Consciousness*. New York, NY: Oxford University Press, 2008.

Smil, Vaclav. *Energy: A Beginner's Guide* (Beginner's Guides). Oxford, England: Oneworld Publications, 2006.

Spence, Christopher. *Global Warming: Personal Solutions for a Healthy Planet*. New York, NY: Palgrave MacMillan, 2005.

Stross, Randall E. *The Wizard of Menlo Park: How Thomas Alva Edison Invented the Modern World*. New York, NY: Three Rivers Press, 2008.

Thornhill, Jan. *This Is My Planet: The Kids' Guide to Global Warming*. Toronto, ON, Canada: Maple Tree Press, 2007.

Wilcox, Charlotte. *Recycling*. North Minneapolis, MN: Lerner Publications, 2007.

ABOUT THE AUTHORS

Nora Clemens is a writer living in New York.

Robert Greenberger, a senior editor at DC Comics, has been writing his entire adult life. His fiction is mainly but not exclusively set in the *Star Trek* universe, where the laws of energy and thermodynamics are scrupulously observed. His nonfiction extends from celebrity interviews to a brief history of Pakistan. He is a lifelong New York Mets fan, making his home in Connecticut with his wife, Deb, and children, Kate and Robbie.

PHOTO CREDITS